KB244188

Finding Psychology

Happy House

About Wise & Wide

- A systematic 6-level English reading program based on Lexile® measures
- Diverse and interesting topics chosen from the elementary curriculums of Korea and English speaking western countries
- Well-written books in various forms including fiction stories, descriptive texts, and classics retold
- The informative but original fiction stories grab your interest, leading to the easy and clear understanding of the educational content.
- Improve thinking skills with solid after-reading activities at all levels of the series.

Wise & Wide is a 6-level English reading program that consists of 60 books and each level is systematically divided by Lexile® measures. The Lexile® Framework for Reading is the most popular reading measuring system in American formal education curriculums and many English programs. Over 20 out of 50 states in the U.S. mark Lexile® measures directly on students' final report cards and over 300 well-known publishers adopt and use Lexile® measures.

Experience many kinds of readings written by professional writers from the U.S. and England. They used interesting topics that were carefully chosen after analyzing elementary curriculums from around the world including Korea, the U.S., England, and Australia among many others. Comprehensive after-reading activities including graphic organizers, speaking tasks, and After-reading Tests are ready for you.

Levels in the series and their corresponding Lexile® measures

Level	Lexile® measures	U.S. Grade
Level 1	Below 200L	Pre K - K
Level 2	190L - 400L	Lower Grade 1
Level 3	350L - 530L	Upper Grade 1
Level 4	420L - 650L	Grade 2
Level 5	520L - 940L	Grade 3 - 4
Level 6	830L - 1070L	Grade 5 - 6

* Smart Readers: Wise & Wide level 1 is applicable to the preschool level in the U.S.
* The source of the relationship between Lexile® measures and U.S. school grades: CCSS(Common Core State Standards) FOR ENGLISH LANGUAGE ARTS, APPENDIX A (2012, which is used by 45 states in the U.S.)

Topic List

	Level 1	Level 2	Level 3	Level 4	Level 5	Level 6
Book 1	Science>Biology: The hibernation of animals Story	Science>Biology: Living and nonliving things Story	Science>Biology: Animals & the Environment: Sea otters Story	Environment> Living with nature: The diver & the persimmon tree Story	Science>Biology> Animal: Amazing animals of the Amazon Story	Science>Biology: Germs, transmitted diseases Story
Book 2	Literature> World classics: Aesop's fables Story	Literature> Traditional fairy tale: Old tales about stones Story	Social Studies> Economy: To run a business to make and save money Story	Science>Biology> Plants: Photosynthesis Story	Science>Earth science Earth's layers, earthquakes, volcanoes, and earth's atmosphere Report	Mathematics> Sequence: The golden ratio & the Fibonacci sequence Story
Book 3	Science>Physics: How shadows are formed Story	Literature> World classics: Peter Pan Story	Science>Scientific technology: Nanobots Story	Literature>Myths: World's creation stories Story	Literature> Legend: The story of King Arthur Story	Literature>Myths: Constellation myths Story
Book 4	Literature> Traditional literature: The Talmud Story	Science>Biology> Animal: Polar bears Story	Science>Biology> Animal: Mountain gorillas Story	Social Studies> Cultural anthropology: Amazing ancient cultures of the world Story	Science> Earth science: Clouds and weather Story	Literature> Human & animals: The friendship between a girl and a horse Story
Book 5	Social Studies> Ethics: Rules in daily life Story	Science>Biology: The five senses Report	Social Studies> Cultural anthropology: Astonishing festivals Report	Art>Music: Stories from two operas Story	Social Studies> World culture & history: The Renaissance Story	Sports> Board sports: Surfing & snowboarding Story
Book 6	Social Studies> World geography & travel: Tourist attractions around the world Story	Science>Biology> Animal: Dinosaurs Story	Science> Astronomy: The solar system Story	Social Studies> People: Three great people who overcame hardships Story	Science>Scientific technology: The wonderful world of robots Report	Art>Music: Composers of the Romantic Era Report
Book 7	Science> Space science: The life of astronauts Report	Social Studies> Cultural anthropology: Mythological monsters from around the world Report	Mathematics> Elementary mathematics: Numbers, measurement, shapes and data Report	Science & Social Studies> Technology & culture: Inventions from around the world Report	Art>Works of art: Famous paintings Report	Social Studies> Human & animals: Animals in action for human Report
Book 8	Social Studies> Cultural anthropology: Various living cultures of the world Story	Art>Music: Instruments in the orchestra Story	Social Studies> Life safety: Learning and using outdoor survival skills Story	Social Studies> History: The California Gold Rush Report	Social Studies & Science> Psychology: Psychology in everyday life Story	Literature> World classics: The Merchant of Venice Story
Book 9	Social Studies> Jobs: Interviews about jobs Report	Science>Scientific technology: Developments in technology in different times Story	Social Studies> Politics>Election: Running for 3rd grade class president Story	Literature> World classics: Stories of Sherlock Holmes Story	Literature> World classics: Adrift in the Pacific Story	
Book 10		Sports>Winter sports: Various aspects of some Winter Olympic sports Report				

* 10 books in each level will be published.

How to Use This Book

•Before Reading

You can easily find the topic and what kind of story you are about to read.

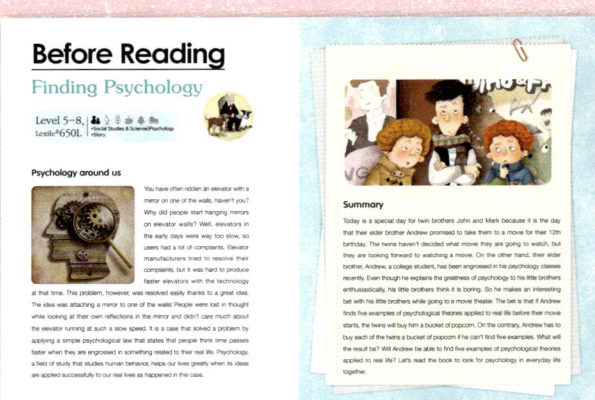

•The text

All the stories were written by professional writers from the U.S. and England, so you will read authentic and appropriate English sentences and expressions in every book in the series.

•Pop Quiz

Check out right away if you understand what you have just read by solving a pop quiz that checks your comprehension.

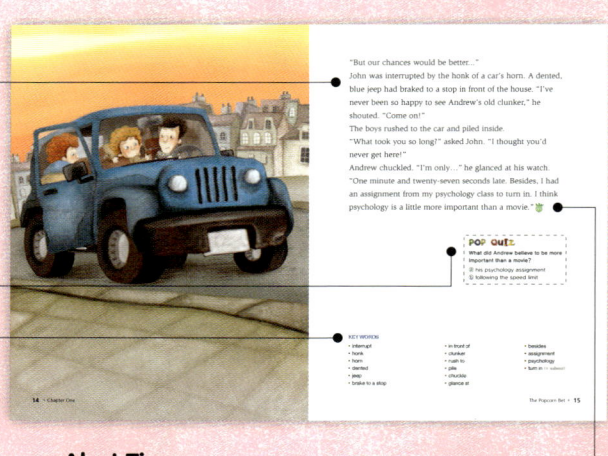

•Key Words

The key words and expressions on each page are listed for you to easily study them.

•Aha! Tips

Download free Korean explanations at *www.ihappyhouse.co.kr* for all of the sentences marked with "Aha!". These explain cultural, scientific, and economic knowledge or they deal with aspects of English such as grammatical structures or idiomatic expressions. There are lots of "Aha! Tips" to help you understand the text.

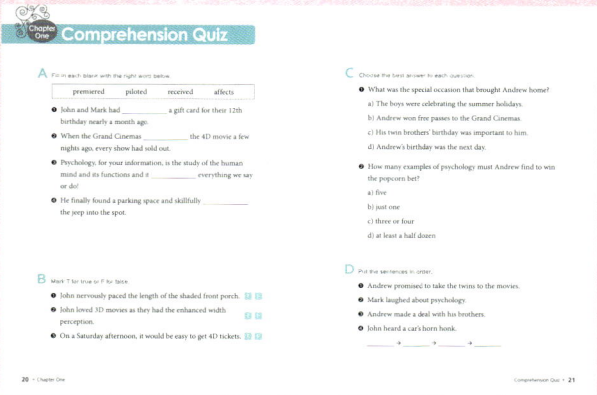

•Comprehension Quiz

After reading one chapter, solve various questions to find out if you fully understand the content.

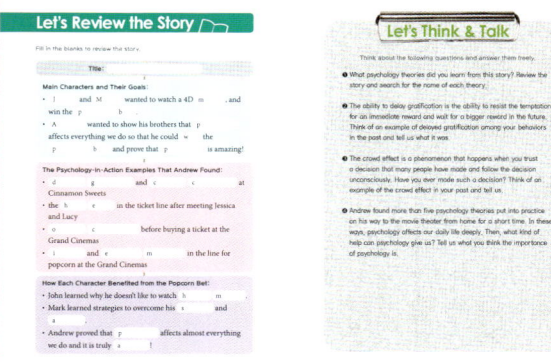

•Let's Review the Story / •Let's Think & Talk

Fill in the blanks in the organizer to summarize the whole story. Express your own thinking and feelings about the story by answering the questions. You can build up logic and reasoning skills for your essay examinations in the future.

Appendix

Audio CD

In the CD audio book form, the texts are read vividly by American professional voice actors. (MP3 files downloaded for free)

After-reading Test

Solve an additionally provided After-reading Test for each book.

The Korean translation, Answer Keys, a Word Quiz, a Word List, and Aha! Tips for each book

You can download them for free at *www.ihappyhouse.co.kr* or *www.darakwon.co.kr*

Before Reading

Finding Psychology

Level 5−8,
Lexile®650L

•Social Studies & Science>Psychology
•Story

Psychology around us

You have often ridden an elevator with a mirror on one of the walls, haven't you? Why did people start hanging mirrors on elevator walls? Well, elevators in the early days were way too slow, so users had a lot of complaints. Elevator manufacturers tried to resolve their complaints, but it was hard to produce faster elevators with the technology at that time. This problem, however, was resolved easily thanks to a great idea. The idea was attaching a mirror to one of the walls! People were lost in thought while looking at their own reflections in the mirror and didn't care much about the elevator running at such a slow speed. It is a case that solved a problem by applying a simple psychological law that states that people think time passes faster when they are engrossed in something related to their real life. Psychology, a field of study that studies human behavior, helps our lives greatly when its ideas are applied successfully to our real lives as happened in this case.

Summary

Today is a special day for twin brothers John and Mark because it is the day that their elder brother Andrew promised to take them to a movie for their 12th birthday. The twins haven't decided what movie they are going to watch, but they are looking forward to watching a movie. On the other hand, their elder brother, Andrew, a college student, has been engrossed in his psychology classes recently. Even though he explains the greatness of psychology to his little brothers enthusiastically, his little brothers think it is boring. So he makes an interesting bet with his little brothers while going to a movie theater. The bet is that if Andrew finds five examples of psychological theories applied to real life before their movie starts, the twins will buy him a bucket of popcorn. On the contrary, Andrew has to buy each of the twins a bucket of popcorn if he can't find five examples. What will the result be? Will Andrew be able to find five examples of psychological theories applied to real life? Let's read the book to look for psychology in everyday life together.

Contents

Finding Psychology

2   About Wise & Wide
4   How to Use This Book
6   Before Reading

Chapter One
10   The Popcorn Bet
20   Comprehension Quiz

Chapter Two
22   Cinnamon Pretzels and Pavlov's Dog
34   Comprehension Quiz

Chapter Three
36   Pretty Girls and a Case of Nerves
48   Comprehension Quiz

Chapter Four
50   Tough Choices and Following the Herd
60   Comprehension Quiz

Chapter Five
62   Movie Decisions and Skinner's Box
74   Comprehension Quiz

Chapter Six
76   Buttery Rewards!
82   Comprehension Quiz

84   Let's Review the Story
85   Let's Think & Talk
86   Let's Review the Story (Answers)
87   After-reading Test

Finding Psychology

Special thanks to Dr. Nicole Harsch, psychology professor at the Decatur campus of Georgia State University.

Chapter One

The Popcorn Bet

John paced the length of the shaded front porch, checking his watch every meter or so. He must have checked his watch a thousand times in the last fifteen minutes! 📖 Aha!

"Where's Andrew?" he asked his twin brother, Mark. "He knows we can't be late for the movie!"

Mark sat on the steps of their house, his long legs stretched out, his arms folded against his chest.

"There are at least a dozen movies scheduled non-stop for the next couple of hours," he said to John. "We're bound to get there in time for one of them."

"But I don't want to see just any old movie." John frowned. "I want to see *Mysterious Island*. If we don't get to the theater soon, the show will sell out!"

John and Mark had received a gift card for their 12th birthday nearly a month ago, and their older brother, Andrew, had promised to take them to the movies.

KEY WORDS

- bet
- pace
- length
- shaded
- porch
- or so
- be late for
- step

- stretch out
- fold
- chest
- at least
- dozen
- scheduled
- non-stop
- (a) couple of

- be bound to + *Verb*
- in time
- frown
- mysterious
- get to (get-got-got/gotten)
- sell out (sell-sold-sold)
- receive
- nearly

▲ watching a 4D movie in the 4D theater

But John had been waiting for something extra special: the opening of the 4D theater! 🌐 He'd watched many 3D movies and loved the enhanced depth perception. But the 4D experience guaranteed that effect as well as other exciting physical effects. John had heard that the *Mysterious Island* included salty sea spray, pitching seats, and even smells! But unfortunately, John was not the only one who'd been waiting to see *Mysterious Island*.

POP QUIZ

What was special about the movie that John wanted to see?

ⓐ The movie, *Mysterious Island*, would start at midnight.
ⓑ The movie, *Mysterious Island*, was a 4D movie.

KEY WORDS

- 4D (= 4 dimensions)
- enhanced
- depth
- perception
- experience

- guarantee
- A as well as B
- exciting
- physical effect
- include

- spray
- pitch
- unfortunately

When the Grand Cinemas premiered the 4D movie a few nights ago, every show had sold out. Now it was Saturday afternoon, and Andrew was nowhere to be seen. If they didn't leave soon, they wouldn't make the show.

"Look," said Mark. "Everyone has the same problem that we do, now that the reserved ticket option isn't available."

The 4D show had been so popular that the online reservation system had crashed!

"We'll just have to take our chances."

KEY WORDS

- premiere
- make (make-made-made)
- show
- now that

- reserved ticket (*cf.* reserve)
- option
- available
- reservation

- crash
- take one's chance (take-took-taken)

"But our chances would be better..."

John was interrupted by the honk of a car's horn. A dented, blue jeep had braked to a stop in front of the house. "I've never been so happy to see Andrew's old clunker," he shouted. "Come on!"

The boys rushed to the car and piled inside.

"What took you so long?" asked John. "I thought you'd never get here!"

Andrew chuckled. "I'm only…" he glanced at his watch. "One minute and twenty-seven seconds late. Besides, I had an assignment from my psychology class to turn in. I think psychology is a little more important than a movie."

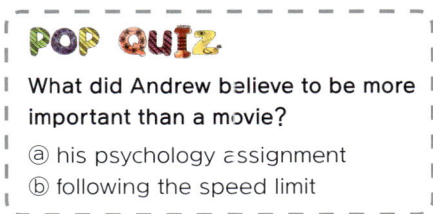

POP QUIZ

What did Andrew believe to be more important than a movie?

ⓐ his psychology assignment
ⓑ following the speed limit

KEY WORDS

- interrupt
- honk
- horn
- dented
- jeep
- brake to a stop

- in front of
- clunker
- rush to
- pile
- chuckle
- glance at

- besides
- assignment
- psychology
- turn in (= submit)

Andrew was in his first year at the university, and the brothers didn't often have the opportunity to see each other. School was a top priority. But a birthday, especially his brothers' birthday, was important, too.

"I don't know about that," said John, buckling his seat belt. "This is going to be an epic movie experience. Much more amazing than psychology."

"Are you kidding?" Andrew shook his head and pulled out of the neighborhood. "Psychology is awesome. The more I learn about it, the more amazing things I find out."

POP QUIZ

What was Andrew's top priority?
ⓐ his university
ⓑ movies

KEY WORDS

- university
- opportunity
- top priority (*cf.* priority)
- buckle one's seat belt
- epic
- amazing

- kid
- shake one's head (shake-shook-shaken)
- pull out (of)
- neighborhood
- awesome

Mark laughed. "Psychology? Amazing? Come on, Andrew. You're the one who's kidding around now."

"Bo-ring," agreed John.

"But it's not boring at all. It truly *is* amazing!" Andrew smiled as he drove. "Psychology, for your information, is the study of the human mind and its functions *and* it affects everything we say or do! You wouldn't believe it."

"You're right about that," said Mark. John nodded.

KEY WORDS

- kid around
- agree
- for one's information
- function
- affect
- nod

Andrew could see the towering lights of the movie theater shining in the distance. He turned into one of the parking lots surrounding the mall where the Grand Cinemas was located.

"All right, let's make a deal," said Andrew.

He finally found a parking space and skillfully piloted the jeep into the spot.

"If I can find five examples of psychology-in-action before our movie starts, you have to buy me a large bucket of popcorn. If I lose, I'll buy each of you a bucket of popcorn."

"A popcorn bet, huh?" Mark turned and looked at John, then he grinned. "We're almost at the theater, you know. We can't lose."

"It's a deal," said John. "And I'll expect extra butter on mine."

KEY WORDS

- towering
- in the distance
- parking lot (*cf.* park / lot)
- surround
- be located

- make a deal (*cf.* deal)
- space
- skillfully
- pilot
- spot

- in action
- lose (lose-lost-lost)
- grin
- expect

A Fill in each blank with the right word below.

premiered	piloted	received	affects

❶ John and Mark had _____ a gift card for their 12th birthday nearly a month ago.

❷ When the Grand Cinemas _____ the 4D movie a few nights ago, every show had sold out.

❸ Psychology, for your information, is the study of the human mind and its functions and it _____ everything we say or do!

❹ He finally found a parking space and skillfully _____ the jeep into the spot.

B Mark T for true or F for false.

❶ John nervously paced the length of the shaded front porch. T F

❷ John loved 3D movies as they had the enhanced width perception. T F

❸ On a Saturday afternoon, it would be easy to get 4D tickets. T F

C Choose the best answer to each question.

❶ What was the special occasion that brought Andrew home?

a) The boys were celebrating the summer holidays.

b) Andrew won free passes to the Grand Cinemas.

c) His twin brothers' birthday was important to him.

d) Andrew's birthday was the next day.

❷ How many examples of psychology must Andrew find to win the popcorn bet?

a) five

b) just one

c) three or four

d) at least a half dozen

D Put the sentences in order.

❶ Andrew promised to take the twins to the movies.

❷ Mark laughed about psychology.

❸ Andrew made a deal with his brothers.

❹ John heard a car's horn honk.

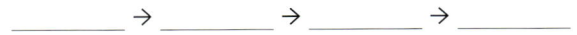

_____ → _____ → _____ → _____

Chapter Two

Cinnamon Pretzels and Pavlov's Dog

Saturdays were always crowded at the mall and so Andrew had been forced to park in a lot on the other side of the Grand Cinemas; the boys had quite a hike ahead of them. John pulled up the collar of his coat and Mark zipped up his jacket. The chill in the air pushed the boys to walk even faster, their older brother Andrew following close on their heels.

KEY WORDS

- cinnamon
- pretzel
- crowded
- be forced to + *Verb*
- on the other side of
- hike
- ahead of

- pull up
- collar
- zip up
- chill
- push
- even
- follow close on one's heels (*cf.* heel)

But Mark paused suddenly and cocked his head.

"You hear that?"

Some music bounced in the air, a song similar to a circus tune playing loudly over a speaker. John grabbed his brother by the arm.

"What are you stopping for? We've got a show time to make."

"But it's the cinnamon pretzel place," said Mark, licking his lips. 🌀 "I'd know that calliope music anywhere."

He closed his eyes and inhaled deeply.

KEY WORDS

- pause
- cock one's head
- bounce

- similar to
- tune
- grab

- lick one's lips
- calliope
- inhale

"I can't smell it yet, but I know it's here. The cinnamon, the sugar, the pretzels… Cinnamon Sweets, that's the name of the place. It's got to be around here somewhere if the music is playing. Come on, guys. I can't be the only one whose mouth is watering. Aren't you craving a cinnamon pretzel right now, too?"

The music swelled to their left, and then Mark spied it, a giant, neon pretzel glowing on a window. Behind the pretzel, two girls in red and white t-shirts with matching hats stood behind a counter, serving pretzels to the line of people waiting. In front of the window, on the sidewalk, another girl in a Cinnamon Sweets uniform stood, holding a white platter. The platter held miniature paper cups, and each cup held a very small portion of a cinnamon pretzel. The scent of cinnamon and butter now floated through the air.

KEY WORDS

- **have got to** + *Verb*
  (= have to, must)
- **water**
- **crave**
- **swell**
- **spy**

- **neon**
- **glow**
- **match**
- **sidewalk**
- **hold** (hold-held-held)
- **platter**

- **miniature**
- **portion**
- **scent**
- **float**

"Mark, you're practically drooling," said John, tugging his brother's arm again. But Mark slipped from his grasp and dashed over to the girl holding the samples. Andrew and John caught him just as he snapped up a pretzel.

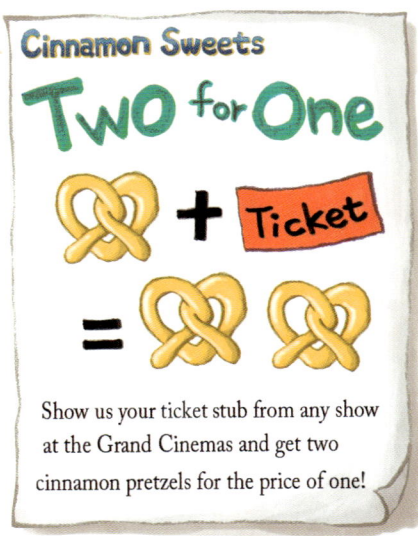

Cinnamon Sweets

Two for One

🥨 + Ticket = 🥨 🥨

Show us your ticket stub from any show at the Grand Cinemas and get two cinnamon pretzels for the price of one!

"Delicious," said Mark, wiping his mouth with the sleeve of his jacket. "Wait just a minute while I run inside and buy a pretzel."

"Wait," said John. "Didn't you see the sign?"

He pointed to a sign on the window. It read, "Show us your ticket stub from any show at the Grand Cinemas and get *two* cinnamon pretzels for the price of one!"

KEY WORDS

- practically
- drool
- tug
- slip
- grasp

- dash over to
- catch (catch-caught-caught)
- snap up
- delicious
- wipe

- sleeve
- point (*cf.* point out)
- read (read-read-read)
- stub

"Thanks for pointing out that delicious deal," said Mark, smiling. "I think I can wait for a cinnamon pretzel, especially if there's a buy-one, get-one free bargain!"

"That's one," said Andrew.

"One what?" John pulled on Mark's arm, and this time, Mark followed.

"One amazing example of psychology," said Andrew. "It's called delayed gratification.  That's the ability to resist an immediate reward in order to wait for a bigger or more enduring reward later."

KEY WORDS

- bargain
- pull on
- delayed (*cf*, delay)
- gratification
- ability
- resist
- immediate
- reward
- in order to + *Verb*
- enduring

"Delayed gratification, huh? Well, you learn something new every day," said John.

He turned to his twin brother. "Don't worry, Mark. It's only one example."

Then he smiled and gave Andrew a playful jab. "You'll need to find four more if you want to win the popcorn bet."

Andrew smiled, too. "And I'm off to a good start. Technically, I'm getting a two-for-one psychology deal with Cinnamon Sweets."

Mark groaned as John hurried along his brothers. "The *movie*, remember?"

"I'll explain while we walk," said Andrew. "We'll begin with a man and his dogs and a little psychological behavior we call 'classical conditioning'."

"Ugh," said John. "It sounds complicated.  What does 'conditioning' mean?"

"It's not that complicated," said Andrew. He pulled out his phone and typed on the keypad, then read aloud. "Here's the definition of classical conditioning: a form of learning in which an organism 'learns' through establishing associations between different events and stimuli."

"Just like I said." John sighed. "Complicated stuff I've never heard before."

POP QUIZ

What was the first amazing example of psychology?

ⓐ delayed thankfulness
ⓑ delayed gratification

KEY WORDS

- playful
- jab
- off to
- technically (*cf.* technical)
- groan
- hurry along
- begin with (begin-began-begun)

- psychological
- behavior
- classical
- conditioning
- complicated
- keypad
- definition

- form
- organism
- establish
- association
- stimulus (*cf.* stimuli)
- sigh
- stuff

▲ Ivan Pavlov

"Wait," said Andrew. "I'll tell you about Pavlov's dog and then you'll understand. Ivan Pavlov was a Russian physiologist who noticed that his dogs would drool whenever they smelled food.  This was an unconditioned response. The dogs didn't learn this behavior; they just automatically responded to the stimulus, that's the food, by drooling. But then he noticed that his dogs would respond the same way when the animals saw the lab assistants, whether they had food or not. So he realized that the dogs had learned a behavior, that they had come to associate food with the lab assistants."

KEY WORDS

- physiologist
- notice
- whenever
- unconditioned
- response
- automatically
- respond

- way
- lab (= laboratory)
- assistant
- whether ~ or not
- realize
- come to + *Verb* (come-came-come)
- associate

"What's the big deal about that?" asked Mark. "I associate food with Mrs. Gold, the cafeteria lady at school." The twins laughed, and so did Andrew. 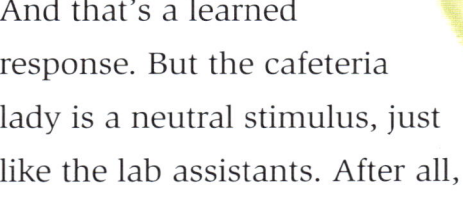 Aha!

"Exactly," said Andrew. "Whenever you see Mrs. Gold, you think of lunch! And that's a learned response. But the cafeteria lady is a neutral stimulus, just like the lab assistants. After all, it's not like Mrs. Gold or the lab assistants are good to eat."

"Ew," said Mark. John shuddered.

POP QUIZ

What animal did Andrew use to explain classical conditioning?

ⓐ Mrs. Gold's cat
ⓑ Pavlov's dog

KEY WORDS

- big deal
- think of

- neutral
- after all

- it's not like
- shudder

"Anyway," continued Andrew, "next, Pavlov decided to use a bell as a neutral stimulus. So every time the dogs were fed, a bell was rung. Guess what happened after a while, when the bell was rung, even if there was no food for the dogs."

John shrugged. "The dogs starved?"

"Oh! I know," said Mark. "The dogs drooled whenever the bell rang! They associated the bell with food, right?"

"Right," said Andrew. "And that's the kind of classical conditioning going on with Cinnamon Sweets."

John nodded. "Yeah, every time Mark hears that music, his mouth waters, even though it's an annoying clown song; it's not even the cinnamon pretzels."

"But it helps that Cinnamon Sweets gives the free samples," said Andrew. "People walking by hear the music and then they get a delicious free cinnamon pretzel. It's classical conditioning, and it works like a charm."

"Okay, fine," said John. "But that's just the second example. And we're almost at the theater."

POP QUIZ

What was the neutral stimulus at Cinnamon Sweets that made people drool?

ⓐ cinnamon and sugar
ⓑ clown song

KEY WORDS

- continue
- feed (feed-fed-fed)
- ring (ring-rang-rung)
- guess
- after a (short) while

- even if (= even though)
- shrug
- starve
- go on with
- annoying

- clown
- walk by
- work
- charm

 A Match each psychology term with the correct example.

❶ neutral stimulus ·

❷ learned response ·

❸ unconditioned response

❹ classical conditioning ·

· a) Dogs drool when food appears.

· b) Pavlov's lab assistants

· c) Pavlov's experiments with dogs and food

· d) Dogs drool when a bell rings.

B Circle the right word for each underlined part.

❶ Some music bounced in the air, a song similar to a circus (<u>tone / tune / turn</u>) playing loudly over a speaker.

❷ It read, "Show us your ticket stub from any show at the Grand Cinemas and get *two* cinnamon pretzels for the (<u>prize / practice / price</u>) of one!"

❸ You'll need to find four more if you want to win the popcorn (<u>beat / vet / bet</u>).

❹ Ivan Pavlov was a Russian (<u>astronaut / physiologist / assistant</u>) who noticed that his dogs would drool whenever they smelled food.

C Choose the best answer to each question.

❶ What was on the platter that the uniformed girl held?

a) paper cups of juice

b) miniature cups of popcorn

c) samples of cheese

d) samples from Cinnamon Sweets

❷ Why did John think that he and Mark would still win the bet?

a) Andrew cheated, getting two psychology examples at Cinnamon Sweets.

b) Andrew had found only two examples, and they were close to the cinema.

c) Mark wouldn't allow Andrew to find any more examples.

d) John knew it would be impossible to find more examples.

D Mark T for true or F for false.

❶ Delayed gratification is the ability to delay something pleasurable.　　T　F

❷ Mark failed when it came to delayed gratification.　　T　F

❸ Andrew wasn't able to find psychology-in-action at Cinnamon Sweets.　　T　F

❹ Mark appreciated a buy-one, get-one-free bargain.　　T　F

Chapter Three

Pretty Girls and a Case of Nerves

The Grand Cinemas was the largest movie theater in town and it looked as if the city's entire population had decided that today would be a great day to watch a movie. There were eight lines leading to the ticket booth to purchase tickets, and each line moved at a snail's pace.

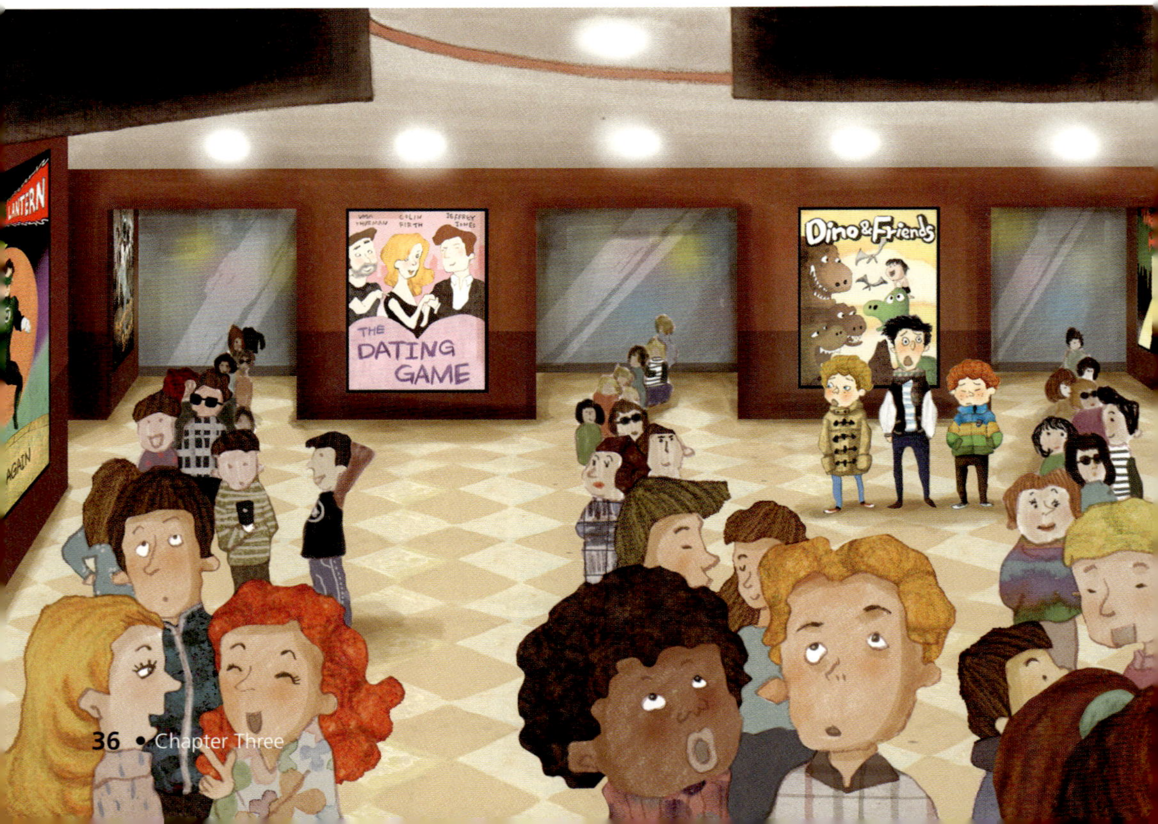

"Quick," said John. He pointed to his right. "Let's get in that line. It's the shortest one."

Andrew started toward the line when Mark grabbed his jacket and pulled his brother back.

"Not that line," he said. "How about over here?"

"But that line is twice as long," said John. "What's wrong with you?"

Mark chewed on his bottom lip. "Nothing," he mumbled. "I just don't want to stand in that line." He wiped his hands on his jeans and stared at the ground.

John looked back at the shortest line and groaned under his breath.

"Oh, no," he said. "It's Jessica Harris and Lucy Brown."

KEY WORDS

- case
- nerves (cf. nerve)
- as if
- entire
- population
- lead to
- ticket office
- purchase
- at a snail's pace
- chew on
- bottom lip (cf. bottom)
- mumble
- stare at
- under one's breath

"What's the problem?" asked Andrew. "They're just a couple of girls."

"*That's* the problem," said John. "They're a couple of girls from our class at school."

Mark ducked behind his twin brother. "Come on," he said. "We can get in another line. *Way* over there." Again, he wiped his sweaty palms across his jeans.

"What are you afraid of?" teased John. "She's not going to bite you."

"I'm not *afraid*," said Mark. "I'm just…"

"All right," said Andrew. "Leave him alone. So Mark's a little shy, a little embarrassed, standing next to a couple of girls he knows. If he had an irrational fear, a phobia about being around girls, then that would be different. That would be another example of a psychological behavior, a social phobia."

KEY WORDS

- duck
- sweaty (*cf.* sweat)
- palm
- be afraid of
- tease
- bite (bite-bit-bitten)
- leave A alone (leave-left-left)
- shy
- embarrassed
- next to
- irrational
- fear
- phobia
- social phobia (*cf.* social)

"Thank goodness, it's just plain shyness," said John.  "We can't afford any more examples."

"Social what?" asked Mark. "What are you talking about now?"

"I'll explain once we get to another line," said Andrew, ushering his brothers far away from the two girls.

"I don't know anything about social phobias," said Mark. "But I know I feel better in this line." He smiled, and his shoulders relaxed. "Whew. That was close."

KEY WORDS

- plain
- shyness
- afford

- usher
- far away (*cf.* far)
- relax

- That was close.

Andrew nodded. "Plenty of us experience anxiety in certain situations. But when a person feels extreme anxiety in a very *specific* situation, and thinks everyone is judging him or her, then it's more than discomfort. It can be a disorder, like social anxiety disorder."

"So it's not a big deal when I'm around Lucy Brown, and I feel like I can't breathe? My palms sweat, my mouth dries up, and my heart pounds like a jackhammer in my chest."

KEY WORDS

- plenty of
- anxiety
- certain
- situation
- extreme
- specific
- judge
- discomfort
- disorder
- breathe
- dry up
- pound
- jackhammer

"I know it feels extreme, but that's just regular anxiety," said Andrew.  "Pretty normal stuff, and you'll probably grow out of it. Or learn strategies to cope with the nervousness. Just like I learned how to deal with my stage fright."

"Remember when you had to give that speech in 10th grade?" John stifled a giggle.

"You turned as white as a sheet," added Mark. "We thought you were going to pass out."

The twins couldn't help it. They burst into laughter.

"All right," said Andrew. "That's enough. I survived, and I learned how to handle the nervousness. The point is, you can change the way you react to certain stressors. You can explore methods to help stop the cycle of fear and anxiety when you're faced with certain situations."

"I wouldn't mind knowing a couple of those tricks," said Mark.

"They're not tricks," said Andrew. "But now that I think about it, there are methods that work like magic." He smiled.

KEY WORDS

- regular
- normal
- grow out of (grow-grew-grown)
- strategy
- cope with (= deal with)
- nervousness
- stage fright (cf. fright)
- give a speech (give-gave-given)
- stifle
- giggle
- pass out

- burst into laughter
- survive
- handle
- react to
- stressor
- explore
- method
- cycle
- be faced with
- not mind + Verb-ing
- trick

"For example, I realized how much I was thinking about what could go *wrong* instead of focusing on what I was doing *right*. I sort of talked to myself, reassuring myself, and that helped me. I also used different relaxation techniques, like deep breathing and meditation. A friend of mine practices yoga, and she believes it's very effective, too. Even now, I follow other healthy habits, like staying away from caffeine and sugar before I give a speech, which would make me even more nervous. (Aha!) And I make sure I'm prepared; I practice saying my speech until I know it so well, I don't need my notes. But mostly, I decided then—and now—that I don't have to be perfect. I just have to be myself."

"That could work for you, Mark. Just be yourself," said John.

KEY WORDS

- go wrong
- instead of
- focus on
- sort of
- talk to oneself
- reassure (= encourage)
- relaxation
- technique
- meditation
- effective
- habit
- stay away from
- caffeine
- make sure
- mostly
- be oneself
- tap

"I don't know," said Mark. "I'd rather have a strategy I could practice. Like you practice saying your speech, Andrew. Do you have any ideas like that?"

Andrew folded his arms and tapped the fingers of one hand against his elbow.

"Let me think… I'll bet you'd feel better if you tried a relaxation technique. Getting the jitters under control—the hammering heart and the butterflies in your stomach—is something you could practice.  You could try deep breathing, like I did, or you could try another technique where you tense a muscle and then relax it. Make a fist and then let it go, and the tension releases."

KEY WORDS

- get A under control
- the jitters
- hammering

- stomach
- tense
- muscle

- make a fist
- tension
- release

"That's easy," said Mark. "But I was thinking you might have an idea for when I have to actually talk to a girl."

"Hmmmm…" Andrew paused then snapped his fingers. "I've got it! You can practice what you're going to say, just like I practice before I give a speech. Start small, maybe just a simple question about a homework assignment, something you know and are comfortable talking about. Or you could have a nice compliment ready. Girls always like when a guy says something nice, right? And of course, you can always offer to help in some way. Be polite. I know it doesn't seem natural, rehearsing what you're going to say or do, but that's how you'll gain confidence. Trust me, Mark, there are simple treatments that work, if *you're* willing to work."

"I hope they work fast," said John. "Lucy's walking over here."

POP QUIZ

What was one idea that Andrew suggested to help Mark talk to a girl?

ⓐ Always ask a girl about her favorite color.
ⓑ Practice what you're going to say.

KEY WORDS

- snap one's fingers
- compliment
- offer
- in some way

- polite
- rehearse
- gain confidence
  (↔ lose confidence)

- trust
- treatment
- be willing to + *Verb*

Comprehension Quiz

A Match each character with the correct explanation to complete the sentence.

❶ Mark •

• a) advised his brother to "just be yourself."

❷ Andrew •

• b) avoided caffeine and sugar before giving a speech.

❸ John •

• c) wanted a coping strategy he could practice.

B Choose the answer that has the correct words for the blanks.

❶ Even though the Grand Cinemas was the _____ theater in town, it was very _____.

a) oldest, beautiful   b) largest, crowded

c) smallest, expensive   d) newest, small

❷ Andrew shared methods he had used that helped him relax, including _____ and _____.

a) drinking plenty of fluids, practicing yoga

b) deep breathing, drinking coffee

c) talking to himself, deep breathing

d) practicing magic tricks, meditation

C Choose the best answer to each question.

1 Why did the twins laugh, remembering their older brother's speech?

a) Andrew forgot the entire speech.

b) Andrew grew so pale that they thought he might pass out.

c) Andrew mispronounced many words that he used.

d) Andrew got the giggles during the speech.

2 What relaxation technique did Andrew suggest Mark try when he's nervous?

a) sitting in a quiet place and reading a good book

b) practicing making a fist and then relaxing

c) eating a handful of chocolate candy bars

d) whistling a happy tune or singing his favorite song

3 Which statement was NOT a suggestion that Andrew gave Mark, when talking to a girl?

a) Discuss something small.

b) Give the girl a compliment.

c) Be polite.

d) Ask about family.

Chapter Four

Tough Choices and Following the Herd

Mark slipped behind Andrew, trying one of the techniques that Andrew mentioned. He made a tight fist and counted to three, then let his fingers relax. Then Mark flexed his arm and let that tension go. He was surprised that his stomach wasn't flipping and tumbling as much as usual.

"Hi, John," said Lucy. "I thought that was you. Hi, Mark," she said, peering around Andrew.

"Hi," mumbled Mark.

His face radiated a pinkish glow, but at least his heart didn't feel like it could jump out of his chest.

"Do you… Um…" Mark cleared his throat. He hadn't really had time to practice what he was going to say!

"Hi," interrupted Andrew. "I'm their brother, Andrew. Nice to meet you."

KEY WORDS

- tough
- herd
- mention
- flex

- flip
- tumble
- as much as usual
- peer

- radiate
- clear one's throat

The girls giggled and Andrew smiled. "So do you have your
tickets already?"

"Yes. We weren't able to get tickets to the 4D movie,
Mysterious Island," said Lucy. "It has sold out. So we had to
choose another one."

John grimaced. "That's the movie we wanted to see, too. I
don't suppose you'd come back next weekend and we could
try again, Andrew?"

Andrew shook his head. "No, I have exams coming up. Why
don't you just pick another movie?"

Mark had been practicing exactly what he wanted to say and now he blurted it out.

"What show are you going to see?" he asked the girls.

"It was so hard to decide," said Jessica. "But everyone in front of us picked *The Dating Game*, so we figured that would be a good choice."

"Ah, the herd effect," said Andrew. "That's number three, if you're counting."

KEY WORDS

- choose
  (choose-chose-chosen)
- grimace
- suppose

- come up
- pick
- blurt out
- dating

- figure
- choice
- herd effect

"Counting what?" asked Lucy.

"Isn't your movie about to start?" John pointed to the flashing sign over their heads.

"Oh!" The girls waded through the crowds to the door. "See you later!" they called over their shoulder. "Enjoy your movie!"

"We are not going to see *The Dating Game*," said John. "I don't care *how* many people think it's a good movie."

"You're sure about that?" teased Andrew. "The herd effect is hard to resist."

"All right," said Mark. "Now I'm interested. What's the herd effect?"

"It's another amazing example of a psychological behavior, a social behavior in which people go along with the crowd. Typically, they don't consider the consequences or think too much about the choice they make. They're just doing what everybody else is doing. And the more people who are following a certain behavior—like buying a ticket to the same show—the more likely it is that other people will do the same. That's the basics of the herd effect."

"You make it sound like something dangerous when you call it that," said Mark. "Like we're all going to get crushed in a stampede."

POP QUIZ

Why did Mark think that the herd effect sounded dangerous?

ⓐ When people followed a crowd, someone might get crushed.

ⓑ A herd of people could wander off and get lost.

KEY WORDS

- be about to + *Verb*
- flash
- wade
- crowd
- go along with
- typically
- consider
- consequence
- likely
- basic
- crush
- stampede

"Well, I don't suppose the herd effect is dangerous, on
its own. But there can be a harmful side to this behavior.
Imagine if someone in your class—let's say it's the most
popular and well-liked guy in your grade—feels threatened
when a new kid arrives at school. So he decides to shut
out the new kid, refuses to include him in any activity, and
doesn't speak to him at all. What do you think happens
next?"

"I know exactly what happens," said Mark. "A few people follow the popular kid first. Then after a short while almost everyone follows along, so almost no one speaks to the new kid. Or at least no one who wants to stay friends with the popular guy."

John shook his head. "I never thought about it like that," he said. "I wonder how many times I've hurt someone by going along with the crowd, without even considering why."

"I told you," said Andrew. "It's a tough behavior to resist. And you'll see applications of it in other fields, like advertising. We call it the 'bandwagon effect' when it pops up there." (Aha!)

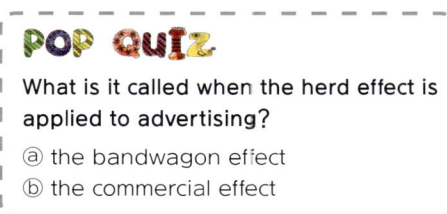

POP QUIZ

What is it called when the herd effect is applied to advertising?

ⓐ the bandwagon effect
ⓑ the commercial effect

KEY WORDS

- on one's own
- harmful
- well-liked
- threatened
- shut out (shut-shut-shut)

- refuse
- wonder
- hurt (hurt-hurt-hurt)
- application
- field

- advertising
- bandwagon
- pop up

"I thought I understood it," said John. "But there's something I don't understand. Why is it called the 'bandwagon effect'?"

"Yeah," said Mark. "What *is* a bandwagon, anyway?"

Andrew smiled. "I don't suppose you see bandwagons much these days. But in the 1800s, political candidates would travel around from town to town, trying to gather support. The candidates would go on these promotional tours riding in these fancy wagons with high sides so they could stand as they traveled. The crowds would follow, jumping up and holding onto the bandwagon, or sometimes literally jumping *into* the wagon."

"Jumping on a wagon?" asked John. "That sounds a little familiar."

"That's where the expression to "jump on the bandwagon" comes from. It's when the voters would crowd around the side of the bandwagon of the candidate that had the largest number of followers. We still use that expression today. It means to go along with the person—or even a product—with the strongest following. So if all of your friends are wearing a particular brand name shoe..."

"Then I want to wear it, too," said Mark, nodding.

"Makes perfect sense," said John, nodding as well. 📖 "But we still need to figure out which movie to watch, now that *Mysterious Island* is out of the question."

POP QUIZ

Where did the expression to "jump on the bandwagon" come from?

ⓐ In the 1800s, political candidates rode in bandwagons.

ⓑ In the 1800s, circus performers traveled in bandwagons.

KEY WORDS

- political candidate
- gather
- support
- go on tour
- promotional
- fancy
- hold onto
- literally
- expression
- come from
- voter
- product
- following
- make sense
- figure out
- out of the question

 A Match each character with his/her behavior to complete the sentence.

❶ Jessica ·

❷ Andrew ·

❸ John ·

❹ Mark ·

· a) felt like he sometimes might have gone along with the crowd.

· b) was influenced by the herd effect when choosing a movie.

· c) explained how the bandwagon effect works.

· d) was finally able to speak to one of the girls.

B Mark T for true or F for false.

❶ The herd effect is a behavior in which people go against the crowd. T F

❷ When caught up in the herd effect, people don't consider the consequences. T F

❸ The more people involved in an activity, the less likely others will follow. T F

❹ The herd effect means everyone will get crushed in a stampede. T F

C Choose the best answer to each question.

❶ Why was Andrew unwilling to return the next weekend to go to the movie?

    a) John did not ask Andrew very nicely.

    b) Andrew needed to study for exams that weekend.

    c) Andrew already had plans with other friends for that weekend.

    d) Andrew thought it would be even more crowded that weekend.

❷ What is the closest definition of a bandwagon?

    a) a wagon for a music concert

    b) an open truck for actors to perform on

    c) a wagon for political candidates to campaign in

    d) a wagon in which only men can ride

D Circle the right word for each underlined part.

❶ In the (<u>1900s</u> / <u>1800s</u>), political candidates traveled from town to town.

❷ Candidates rode in wagons with high sides so they could (<u>stand</u> / <u>sit</u>).

❸ Crowds followed the wagons, sometimes jumping (<u>under</u> / <u>into</u>) the wagons.

❹ Voters followed the candidate with the (<u>largest</u> / <u>smallest</u>) number of followers.

Chapter Five

Movie Decisions and Skinner's Box

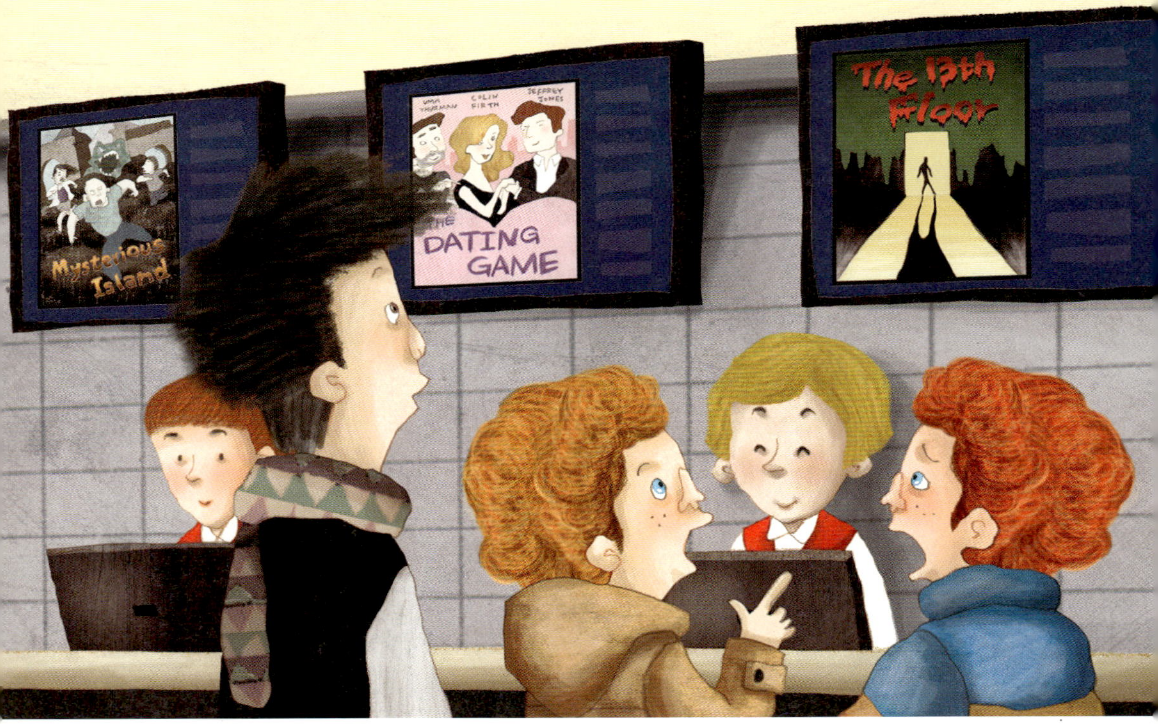

The boys turned to check out the movie posters on the screens inside the theater lobby.

"I don't have a preference," said Andrew. "Choose what you like."

"None of those romance movies like *The Dating Game*," said John.

"Agreed," said Mark. "And no animation. I'm not in the mood for cartoons."

"I'm not, either." said John.

"That leaves…" Mark paused. "Look! It's *The 13th Floor*! I didn't know that movie was still playing. Let's watch that one!"

"The horror movie?" asked Andrew. "It's okay with me if it's okay with the two of you."

"It's definitely *not* okay with me," said John. "No way will I watch a horror movie."

"Uh-oh," said Mark. "Look, that other movie was nearly two years ago. Can't you forget about it? I've been dying to see *The 13th Floor*." Aha!

KEY WORDS

- decision
- lobby
- have a preference (for/of) (*cf.* preference)
- be not in the mood for
- cartoon (= animation)

- either
- be okay with
- definitely
- no way
- be dying to + *Verb*

"That's just it," said John. "I'll never forget that other movie."

"This is an interesting development," said Andrew. "What other movie?"

"It was one of those late night B horror movies. You know the kind, low budget movies where the special effects are

terrible and all the actors are overly dramatic. Mom let us stay up to watch it, but John got scared. And now he won't watch any horror movies."

"It's not because they scare me. It's because you made fun of me as we watched!"

KEY WORDS

- That's just it.
- development
  (cf. develop)
- budget

- special effect
- terrible
- overly
- dramatic

- stay up
- scare
- make fun of

64 • Chapter Five

"Just as I suspected," said Andrew. "That sounds like operant conditioning to me, boys. Aha! I believe that's number four in the psychology examples."

"Oh, no. Not another one," groaned Mark.

"Oh, yes," said Andrew. "Don't you want to know how it works?"

"No, thanks," said Mark.

"Yes," said John.

Andrew smiled. "John wins." He pulled out his cell phone and typed onto the keypad.

"Here it is. Operant conditioning: a method of learning that occurs through reinforcements and punishments for behaviors. It encourages the subject to associate desirable or undesirable outcomes with certain behaviors."

POP QUIZ

Why did John refuse to watch the movie that Mark wanted to watch?

ⓐ It was a movie with too much violence.
ⓑ He knew his brother would make fun of him.

KEY WORDS

- suspect
- operant conditioning (*cf.* operant)
- occur
- reinforcement
- punishment

- encourage
- subject
- desirable (↔ undesirable)
- outcome

Mark sighed. "More confusing technical terms. What does that have to do with us going to the horror movie?"

"Everything," said Andrew. "And I can explain it in a simple way. When John watched a horror movie, sure, it scared him. But that was an involuntary response. When *you* made fun of him," Andrew pointed at Mark, "it was like a punishment for his behavior. So now, John doesn't want to watch a horror movie again. He doesn't want you harassing him!"

KEY WORDS

- confusing
- term
- have to do with
- involuntary
- harass

"Oh, I get it," said John. "I learned something important that night. Namely, that if I watched a horror movie, I'd pay for it with Mark's teasing through the whole movie. I'd say that's an undesirable outcome. Wouldn't you, Mark?"

"Well, yeah. But it's not fair. I really *enjoyed* watching the horror movie. I like being scared, as long as it's on a screen."

"That's operant conditioning, too," said Andrew. "You experienced *positive* reinforcement from horror, so you're likely to want the experience again. B. F. Skinner had it all figured out."

KEY WORDS

- namely
- pay for
- fair
- as long as
- positive
- be likely to + *Verb*

"Who's B. F. Skinner?" asked Mark.  "Wait. I bet I know. He was some kind of brilliant psychologist, right?"

"Yes and no," said Andrew. "He wasn't very interested in understanding the human psyche, why our minds work the way they do. He was a strict behaviorist."

"A behaviorist? Is that someone who watches other people's behavior?" asked John.

"Well, that's putting it in very simple terms, but yes, Skinner definitely was interested in animal behavior. He studied rats in one of his first jobs as a psychology student, working in a biology lab at Harvard University."

POP QUIZ

Who was the famous behaviorist that Andrew mentioned?

ⓐ Lucy Brown

ⓑ B. F. Skinner

KEY WORDS

- brilliant
- be interested in
- psyche
- strict
- behaviorist
- put (put-put-put)
- rat
- biology

Andrew nudged the boys to move forward in the line. "He had a knack for making stuff—he liked building Rube Goldberg contraptions, those complicated devices with all kinds of chain reactions in order to perform an easy task— so he built a special box that the rats could use. Pushing a button or flipping a lever would reward the rat for certain behaviors. He was very good at developing these boxes, and their designs were huge improvements, so eventually they became known as 'Skinner Boxes.'  He moved to the University of Minnesota and continued his research into behavior using pigeons."

KEY WORDS

- nudge
- a knack for
- contraption
- device
- chain reaction
- perform
- lever

- be good at (↔ be poor at)
- huge
- improvement
- eventually
- become known as (become-became-become)
- pigeon

"Pigeons? Look, I understand the rats," said Mark. "I've seen rats run through mazes. I could even see where hamsters could punch a button to get food. But pigeons? Using those birds doesn't make sense."

Andrew chuckled. "It does when you consider that outside his office window were lots of pigeons, roosting. He had an ample supply! And training birds is just as easy as working with rats, if you have the right food. In fact, pigeons became his favorite subjects and led him to develop his theories about operant conditioning."

"Oh, yeah," said John. "Isn't operant conditioning where we started?"

Andrew nodded. "It sure is. He trained the pigeons, influenced by a psychologist named Edward Thorndike and the work he'd done with the 'law of effects'.  It all comes down to this idea: actions that are followed by reinforcement are likely to occur again. On the other hand, actions that are punished are far less likely to occur again."

▲ Edward Thorndike

"I think Mr. Skinner and his buddy, Mr. Thorndike, were one hundred percent correct," said John. "I'd rather not have to deal with Mark and his annoying remarks today! And that's why we're not going to watch *The 13th Floor*."

KEY WORDS

- maze
- roost
- ample
- supply
- in fact
- lead A to + *Verb* (lead-led-led)
- theory

- influence
- come down to
- on the other hand
- buddy
- remark
- that is why

Mark scowled and scanned the posters again. There was only one group of people ahead of them buying tickets. He needed to choose fast!

"What about *The Green Lantern Strikes Again*? We both liked the first movie..."

"That's probably a good choice," agreed John. "I see quite a few people heading into that movie."

"So the herd effect strikes again." Mark sighed. "I'm beginning to think we might lose the popcorn bet."

"Not a chance," said John. 📖 "We've almost *made it*!"

POP QUIZ

What was the movie that the boys finally chose to watch?

ⓐ *The Green Lantern Strikes Again*
ⓑ *The 13th Floor*

KEY WORDS

- **scowl** (= grimace)
- **scan**
- **strike** (strike-struck-struck/stricken)

- **quite a few** (= many, much)
- **head into**
- **make it**

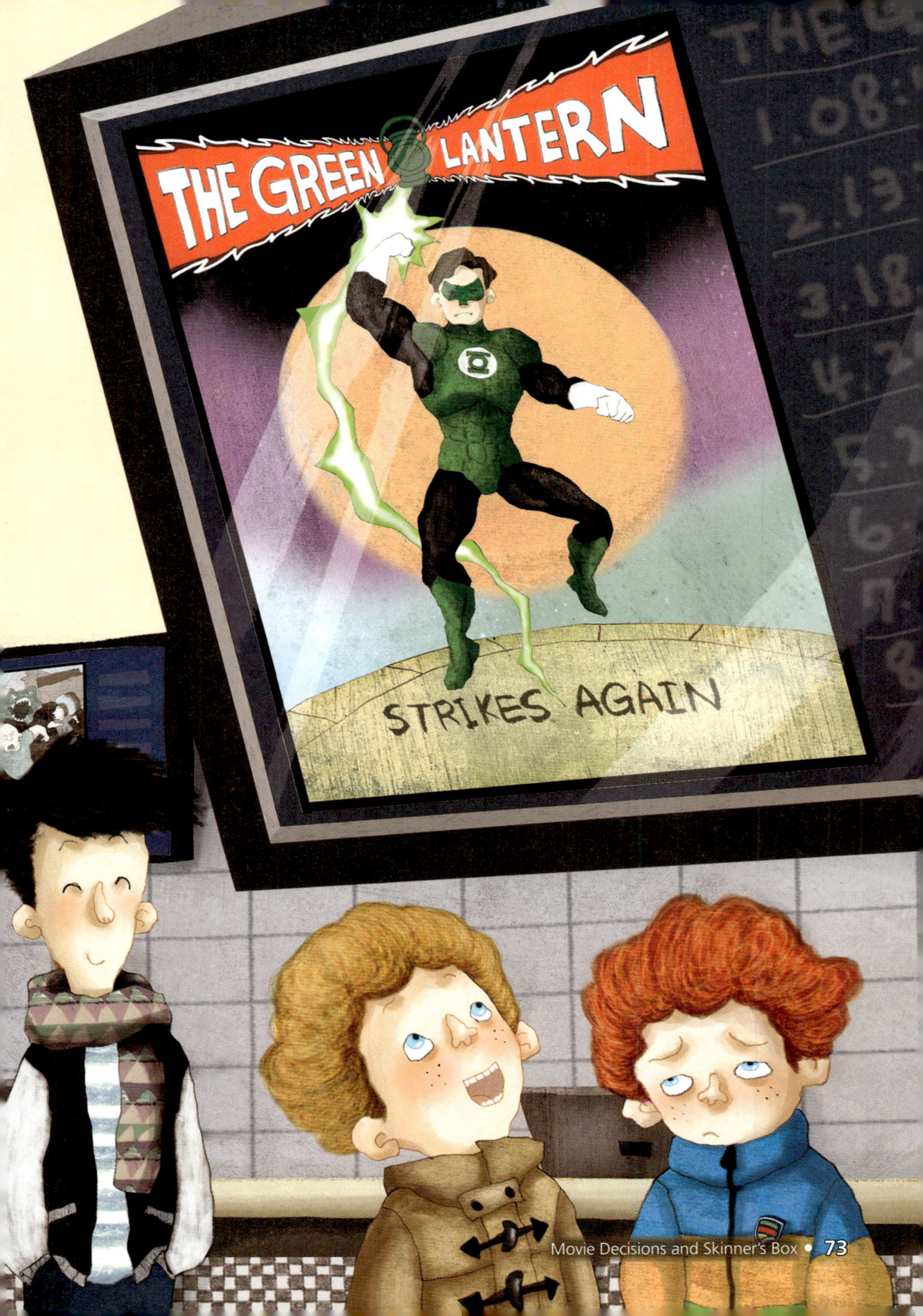
THE GREEN LANTERN
STRIKES AGAIN

Chapter Five

Comprehension Quiz

A Match each given word with its correct explanation.

❶ B movie •

❷ behaviorist •

❸ Edward Thorndike •

❹ Rube Goldberg machine •

❺ Skinner boxes •

• a) experimental boxes with rewards for rats

• b) low budget movie with bad special effects

• c) a contraption with chain reactions

• d) developed the "law of effects"

• e) B. F. Skinner

B Mark T for true or F for false.

❶ Andrew found the fourth example of psychology.　　T　F

❷ The twins thought *The Dating Game* might be a good choice.　　T　F

❸ John refused to watch horror movies.　　T　F

❹ Mark was excited for a chance to see *The 13th Floor*.　　T　F

C

Choose the best answer to each question.

❶ What was the positive reinforcement that Mark received when watching horror movies?

a) The movie scared him, and Mark liked being frightened.

b) The movie made Mark laugh, even though it was scary.

c) Mark really enjoyed watching his brother John.

d) Mark liked the special effects in the horror movie he saw.

❷ When crowds were getting into the same movie line, what behavior struck again?

a) operant conditioning   b) delayed gratification

c) the herd effect   d) classical conditioning

D

Circle the right word for each underlined part.

❶ Mark (<u>didn't</u> / did) know that *The 13th Floor* was still playing.

❷ John and Mark (<u>were</u> / weren't) happy when Andrew found another example.

❸ John (<u>couldn't</u> / could) forget a horror movie he'd watched.

❹ Now, John (won't / <u>will</u>) watch horror movies.

Chapter Six

Buttery Rewards!

At last, the boys completed their Grand Cinemas choice! They had tickets for what they hoped would be a good movie, and all they needed to do was get their popcorn. Unfortunately, there was another long line. That meant they'd have another long wait.

But the twins didn't mind. They'd limited Andrew and his amazing psychology examples to four; they were feeling more than satisfied.

"I've always wanted to get the extra large bucket of popcorn," said Andrew, scanning the sign above the concession stand. "And now I can afford it. Or rather, *you* can afford it." Andrew chuckled.

"Not so fast, Andrew. You'll have to wait till next time," said John.

"Yeah," said Mark. "*We* won the bet. You owe *us* two buckets of popcorn."

KEY WORDS

- buttery
- complete
- limit
- satisfied
- concession stand
- Not so fast!
- owe A B

Extra
Large

"I don't think so, boys," said Andrew. "I was saving extrinsic and intrinsic motivation for just the right moment."

"You have got to be kidding," groaned Mark. "It's not possible."

"Oh, but it is. I tried to tell you that psychology explains everything we do, including what motivates our behaviors. That's where intrinsic and extrinsic motivation comes in. Take me, for example. I came home today because I wanted to see my little brothers and take you to the movies. Do you want to know why?"

"That's no big mystery," said Mark. "It was because of our birthday a few weeks ago."

"Yeah," said John. "And because we're awesome brothers and you wanted to do something awesome for us."

POP QUIZ

What was Andrew saving for just the right moment?

ⓐ the idea of extrinsic and intrinsic motivation
ⓑ tickets for the 4D movie

KEY WORDS

- save
- extrinsic (↔ intrinsic)
- motivation (*cf.* motivate)
- possible (↔ impossible)

- including
- come in
- mystery
- because of

- absolutely
- equal
- at work

Andrew nodded. "You know what? That's absolutely true. Intrinsic motivation is when you do something for its own reward. The good feeling comes from inside, that's the intrinsic part."

"Inside equals intrinsic," said Mark. "Got it. So you did something nice, just because we're your brothers."

"Are you sure Mom didn't pay you to come home and take us to the movies?" asked John.

Andrew laughed. "No, Mom didn't pay me. But if she had, that would be *extrinsic* motivation at work. Do you know what extrinsic means?"

John shook his head. "I don't think I want to know, either."

Andrew continued. "Extrinsic means external, something that operates from the outside. So extrinsic motivation refers to a behavior that's driven by an external reward. Like when we do something because there's a pay-off for us. Maybe we study hard to get a good grade, or…"

"Yikes. I see where this is going," said John. "Or a big brother points out all kinds of amazing psychology examples so he'll win a popcorn bet."

Andrew laughed. "I'm afraid so, boys. It's time to pay off your debt."

"But think of all we learned today," said John. "Wouldn't a bucket of popcorn positively reinforce the lesson?"

"Yeah, we're practically psychology experts now," said Mark. "That has to be worth a bucket of popcorn!"

KEY WORDS

- external
- operate
- refer to
- drive
- pay-off (*cf.* pay off)
- yikes
- debt

- positively
- expert
- be worth
- treat
- step up to
- forget (forget-forgot-forgotten)

Andrew laughed again. "Okay, okay. I'll treat this time. As long as you both agree I won the bet."

The twins shrugged and stepped up to the counter.

"Two buckets of popcorn, please," said Mark.

John grinned. "And don't forget the extra butter!"

POP QUIZ

In the end, which of the brothers actually won the popcorn bet?

ⓐ Andrew
ⓑ John and Mark

A Match each character with the correct explanation to complete the sentence.

❶ Mom •   • a) came home for the day.

❷ John •   • b) solved the mystery about intrinsic motivation.

❸ Mark •   • c) did not pay anyone to come home.

❹ Andrew •   • d) knew he was an awesome brother.

B Circle the right word for each underlined part.

❶ They'd limited Andrew and his amazing psychology (experiments / examples / homework) to four.

❷ I was (spending / searching / saving) extrinsic and intrinsic motivation for just the right moment.

❸ The good feeling comes from (inside / outside / indoor), that's the intrinsic part.

❹ Extrinsic means (except / external / internal), something that operates from the outside.

C Choose the best answer to each question.

❶ Why were the twins unconcerned about another wait?

a) They knew they had plenty of time before the movie started.

b) They'd buy candy and snacks to pass the time.

c) They had comfortable chairs to sit in.

d) They felt like they had won the popcorn bet.

❷ What was Andrew's extrinsic motivation when he accepted the psychology bet?

a) He would get a free ticket to the movie.

b) He would win a bucket of popcorn.

c) He would get a good grade on his exam.

d) He would get to spend time with his brothers.

D Put the sentences in order.

❶ The twins finally chose what to watch.

❷ Andrew came up with two more psychology examples.

❸ Andrew bought two buckets of popcorn.

❹ The boys had to stand in a long line.

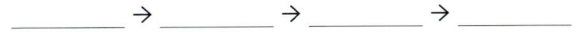
_____ → _____ → _____ → _____

Let's Review the Story

Fill in the blanks to review the story.

Title: _____

Main Characters and Their Goals:

- J _____ and M _____ wanted to watch a 4D m _____ , and win the p _____ b _____ .

- A _____ wanted to show his brothers that p _____ affects everything we do so that he could w _____ the p _____ b _____ and prove that p _____ is amazing!

The Psychology-in-Action Examples That Andrew Found:

- d _____ g _____ and c _____ c _____ at Cinnamon Sweets

- the h _____ e _____ in the ticket line after meeting Jessica and Lucy

- o _____ c _____ before buying a ticket at the Grand Cinemas

- i _____ and e _____ m _____ in the line for popcorn at the Grand Cinemas

How Each Character Benefited from the Popcorn Bet:

- John learned why he doesn't like to watch h _____ m _____ .
- Mark learned strategies to overcome his s _____ and a _____ .

- Andrew proved that p _____ affects almost everything we do and it is truly a _____ !

Let's Think & Talk

Think about the following questions and answer them freely.

❶ What psychology theories did you learn from this story? Review the story and search for the name of each theory.

❷ The ability to delay gratification is the ability to resist the temptation for an immediate reward and wait for a bigger reward in the future. Think of an example of delayed gratification among your behaviors in the past and tell us what it was.

❸ The crowd effect is a phenomenon that happens when you trust a decision that many people have made and follow the decision unconsciously. Have you ever made such a decision? Think of an example of the crowd effect in your past and tell us.

❹ Andrew found more than five psychology theories applied to real life on his way to the movie theater for a short time. In these ways, psychology affects our daily life deeply. Then, what kind of help can psychology give us? Tell us what you think the importance of psychology is.

Let's Review the Story

Title: Finding Psychology

Main Characters and Their Goals:

- John and Mark wanted to watch a 4D movie , and win the popcorn bet .
- Andrew wanted to show his brothers that psychology affects everything we do so that he could win the popcorn bet and prove that psychology is amazing!

The Psychology-in-Action Examples That Andrew Found:

- delayed gratification and classical conditioning at Cinnamon Sweets
- the herd effect in the ticket line after meeting Jessica and Lucy
- operant conditioning before buying a ticket at the Grand Cinemas
- intrinsic and extrinsic motivation in the line for popcorn at the Grand Cinemas

How Each Character Benefited from the Popcorn Bet:

- John learned why he doesn't like to watch horror movies .
- Mark learned strategies to overcome his shyness and anxiety .
- Andrew proved that psychology affects almost everything we do and it is truly amazing !

Smart Readers: **Wise** & **Wide**

After-reading **Test**

- Finding Psychology
- Level 5
- 28 Questions

(Vocabulary 6 / Reading Comprehension 16 /

Sentence Structure & Grammar 6)

Finding Psychology After-reading Test

1. If there are a dozen movies scheduled, how many movies will be shown?
    ① twelve
    ② fewer than ten
    ③ twenty
    ④ fifteen

2. What does "cope with" mean?
    ① to deal effectively with something difficult
    ② to ignore completely
    ③ to turn around a situation
    ④ to believe something will get better

3. What does "blurted" mean in the following sentence?

    > Mark had been practicing exactly what he wanted to say and now he <u>blurted</u> it out.

    ① whispered
    ② shouted very loudly
    ③ spoke suddenly
    ④ talked in a calm and reassuring manner

4. What is the proper word for the blank?

    > When *Mysterious Island* _____, every show had sold out.

    ① guaranteed
    ② threatened
    ③ rehearsed
    ④ premiered

5. What is the common word for the two blanks?

- But we still need to figure _____ which movie to watch.
- He pulled _____ his cell phone and typed onto the keypad.

① on   ② to

③ out   ④ with

6. What are the proper words for the blanks?

- It's because you made fun _____ me as we watched!
- So extrinsic motivation refers _____ a behavior that's driven by an external reward.

① to − as

② of − with

③ of − to

④ with − of

7. Why did the brothers NOT have an opportunity to see each other often?

① Andrew was in his first year at the university.

② Andrew worked part-time after school.

③ The twins lived very far away from Andrew.

④ The twins were always busy with after-school activities.

8. Why did Mark think that he and John would win the bet?

① He figured Andrew was just kidding about psychology.

② Time would run out before Andrew could find examples.

③ Mark loved popcorn and would do whatever it took to win.

④ He knew John had a trick to win the bet.

9. Why did John think the definition of classical conditioning was complicated?
   ① Andrew had to call his professor to get information.
   ② The definition contained an unfamiliar word.
   ③ It took Andrew five minutes to explain the words.
   ④ John thought that only a college student could understand it.

10. According to Pavlov, what was the unconditioned response of his dogs to food?
    ① The dogs would bark when they smelled food.
    ② The dogs would drool when they smelled food.
    ③ The dogs would drool when a bell rang.
    ④ The dogs would run away when food was offered.

11. According to Pavlov, what behavior did the dogs learn?
    ① The dogs learned that Pavlov would not give them water.
    ② The dogs soon associated food with Pavlov.
    ③ The dogs learned to associate the lab assistants with food.
    ④ The dogs figured out how to get more food from Pavlov.

12. What was the classical conditioning that occurred with Cinnamon Sweets and Mark?
    ① Every time Mark heard calliope music, his mouth watered.
    ② Every time Mark smelled cinnamon, he wanted to go to Cinnamon Sweets.
    ③ Whenever Mark saw a pretzel, he heard calliope music.
    ④ Because Mark loved cinnamon pretzels, he loved clown music, too.

13. Who are Jessica Harris and Lucy Brown?
    ① two girls from Mark and John's class
    ② Andrew's friends from university
    ③ the stars of the 4D movie, *Mysterious Island*
    ④ the two girls whom John invited to the movies

14. What advice did Andrew have that would help Mark with his shyness?
    ① He told Mark to stay far away from girls.
    ② He told Mark to find John whenever he was nervous.
    ③ He told Mark that he could change the way he reacts.
    ④ He advised Mark to stay home from school.

15. When the girls explain why they chose the movie they will watch, Andrew called it an example of _____.
    ① the stampede effect
    ② low of effects
    ③ Skinner Syndrome
    ④ the herd effect

16. If you were "jumping on the bandwagon", what action might you take?
    ① All your friends are going shopping and you play basketball.
    ② Your three best friends collect stamps and you collect coins.
    ③ Everyone in your class has a blue notebook and you buy a blue notebook.
    ④ Many of your teammates have white socks so you get white socks with stripes.

17. What kind of movie was *The 13th Floor*?
    ① romance   ② horror
    ③ comedy   ④ thriller

18. Which statement describes a characteristic of a B movie?
    ① B movies are always on late in the afternoon.
    ② B movies have low budgets but great special effects.
    ③ B movies always have celebrities acting in them.
    ④ B movies often feature overly dramatic actors.

19. Which is NOT true about operant conditioning and John's past experience?
    ① When John watched a horror movie, he had an involuntary response.
    ② John won't watch horror movies with Mark, but not because he's afraid.
    ③ Being teased during the horror movie was undesirable for John.
    ④ Being harassed by Mark was actually pleasant for John.

20. What made pigeons a good animal for experiments?
    ① Pigeons will always fly back to a trainer.
    ② Pigeons are easily trained with the right food.
    ③ Pigeons can be found all over the world.
    ④ Pigeons work well with rats and hamsters.

21. What is the best definition for intrinsic motivation?
① When people do something knowing they will be paid.
② When people do something because it makes them feel good.
③ When people do something even though they don't want to do it.
④ When people do something because it's easy and cheap.

22. Why did the twins think that Andrew should buy the popcorn?
① They had not listened to all of Andrew's psychology examples.
② It would reinforce what they had learned about psychology.
③ They didn't think all of the psychology examples should count.
④ They had not been serious about a popcorn bet, after all.

※ Choose the wrong part of each sentence. (23~24)

23.
But that line is two as long.
  ①   ②   ③   ④

24.
I've been dying seeing *The 13th Floor*.
①   ②   ③   ④

25. What is the correct sentence?
① The twins laughed, and so did Andrew.
② The twins laughed, and so was Andrew.
③ The twins laughed, and so were Andrew.
④ The twins laughed, and so does Andrew.

※ Choose the correct word for each blank. (26~28)

26. The more I learn about it, the _____ amazing things I find out.

① better
③ many

② rather
④ more

27. It sounds _____.

① complicate
③ complicacy

② complicated
④ complication

28. I wouldn't mind _____ a couple of those tricks.

① to know
③ known

② knew
④ knowing

⊹ You can download the answer keys at www.ihappyhouse.co.kr

Cathy C. Hall

Cathy C. Hall graduated with a broadcasting degree, working in the radio industry as a news reporter and commercial copywriter before going back to school to earn English certification. She spent a decade in education, teaching preschoolers, middle schoolers, and high schoolers. Now, she's a full-time freelance writer, with stories, essays, and poems in publications for both children and adults. Her byline appears in books like *Uncle John's Facts To Annoy Your Teacher*, *Chicken Soup for the Soul's Think Positive for Kids*, *Cup of Comfort for Dog Lovers*, and many more.

 **Smart Readers Wise & Wide** 5-8

Finding Psychology

Written by Cathy C. Hall
Illustrated by Gyeonga Jeong

First Published in September 2016

Editorial Manager: Juyon Choi
Editors: Juyon Choi, Myungjin Kim, Kyunghee Jang, Jiyeong Park
Designer: Eunhee Lee
Cover Designer: Eunhee Lee

Published and distributed by

 Happy House

Darakwon Bldg., 64-1 Jandari-ro, Mapo-gu, Seoul, Korea 04031
Tel: 82-2-736-2031(ext. 250)   Fax: 82-2-732-2037
Homepage: www.ihappyhouse.co.kr
Publisher: Kyudo Chung

Copyright © Darakwon Publishing Company 2016
English Edition published 2016, by arrangement with Darakwon, by Happy House
English Edition Copyright © 2016, Happy House

All rights reserved. No part of this publication may be reproduced, stored in
a retrieval system, or transmitted in any form or by any means, electronic,
mechanical, photocopying or otherwise, without the prior consent of the
copyright owner. Refund after purchase is possible only according to the company
regulations. Contact the above telephone number for any inquiries.
Consumer damages caused by loss, damage, etc. can be compensated
according to the consumer dispute resolution standards announced by the Korea
Fair Trade Commission. An incorrectly collated book will be exchanged.

ISBN: 978-89-6653-493-7 18740 / 978-89-6653-156-1 18740(set)

[Components]
• 1 Audio CD (Recording Studio: Aram)
• Answer Keys & Korean Translation: Free download at www.ihappyhouse.co.kr